BUILT FOR SPEED
AIRCRAFT

IAN GRAHAM

 Belitha Press

First published in the UK in 1997 by
Belitha Press Limited
London House, Great Eastern Wharf,
Parkgate Road, London SW11 4NQ

ISBN 1 85561 711 0

British Library Cataloguing in Publication Data
for this book is available from the British Library.

Printed in Hong Kong

Editor: Stephanie Bellwood
Designer: Dave Goodman
Series design: Helen James
Illustrator: Tom Connell
Picture researcher: Diana Morris
Consultants: Lindsay Peacock
              Ann Robinson
Additional diagram (p17) by Kevin Lyles

Picture acknowledgements:
Airbus Industrie: 9. Air France/TRH Pictures: 15. British Aerospace/TRH Pictures: 16.
British Airways/TRH Pictures: 26. Ian Graham: 28t, 29t. Military Picture Library: 25.
NASA/TRH Pictures: 13, 14, 20. E. Nevill/TRH Pictures: 6, 18. Northrop Grumman
Corp/TRH Pictures: 28c. Quadrant Picture Library: 11, 21, 23, 24, 27.
Rolls-Royce plc: 8, 10. Sikorsky/TRH Pictures: 22. TRH Pictures: 19. USAF/TRH
Pictures: 17, 29c. US National Archives/TRH Pictures: 12. US Navy/TRH Pictures: 7.

Words in **bold** are explained in the glossary on pages 30 and 31.

Contents

The quest for speed

Ever since the first person climbed on a horse and galloped into the distance, people have been finding new ways of travelling further and faster. In 1903 the Wright brothers made the world's first powered flight. Since then we have found ways to fly halfway round the world at twice the **speed of sound** and double the height of Mount Everest in just a few hours. And aircraft design is still changing fast.

▲ The first aeroplane
The first successful aeroplane was the Wright Flyer, built by Orville and Wilbur Wright. On 17 December 1903 the plane took off under its own power for the first time. It flew 30 metres and reached a speed of 48 km/h.

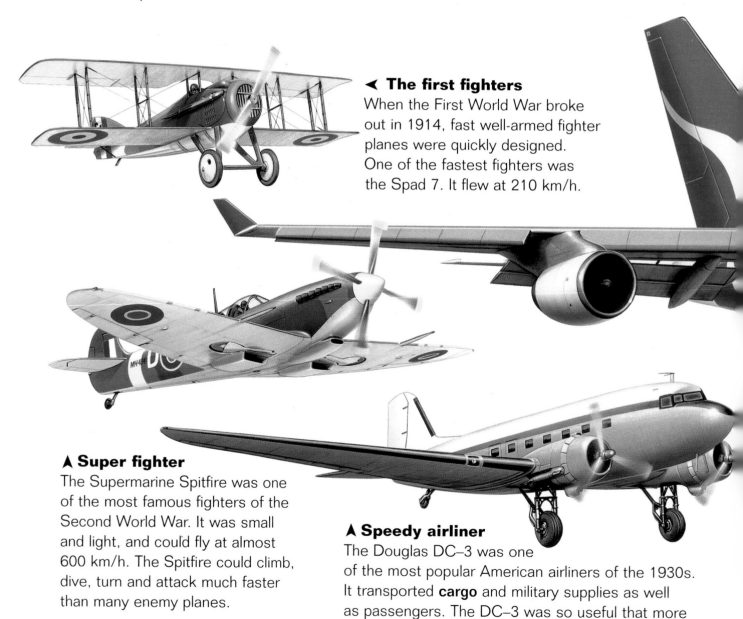

◄ The first fighters
When the First World War broke out in 1914, fast well-armed fighter planes were quickly designed. One of the fastest fighters was the Spad 7. It flew at 210 km/h.

▲ Super fighter
The Supermarine Spitfire was one of the most famous fighters of the Second World War. It was small and light, and could fly at almost 600 km/h. The Spitfire could climb, dive, turn and attack much faster than many enemy planes.

▲ Speedy airliner
The Douglas DC–3 was one of the most popular American airliners of the 1930s. It transported **cargo** and military supplies as well as passengers. The DC–3 was so useful that more than 13 000 were built. It flew at up to 350 km/h.

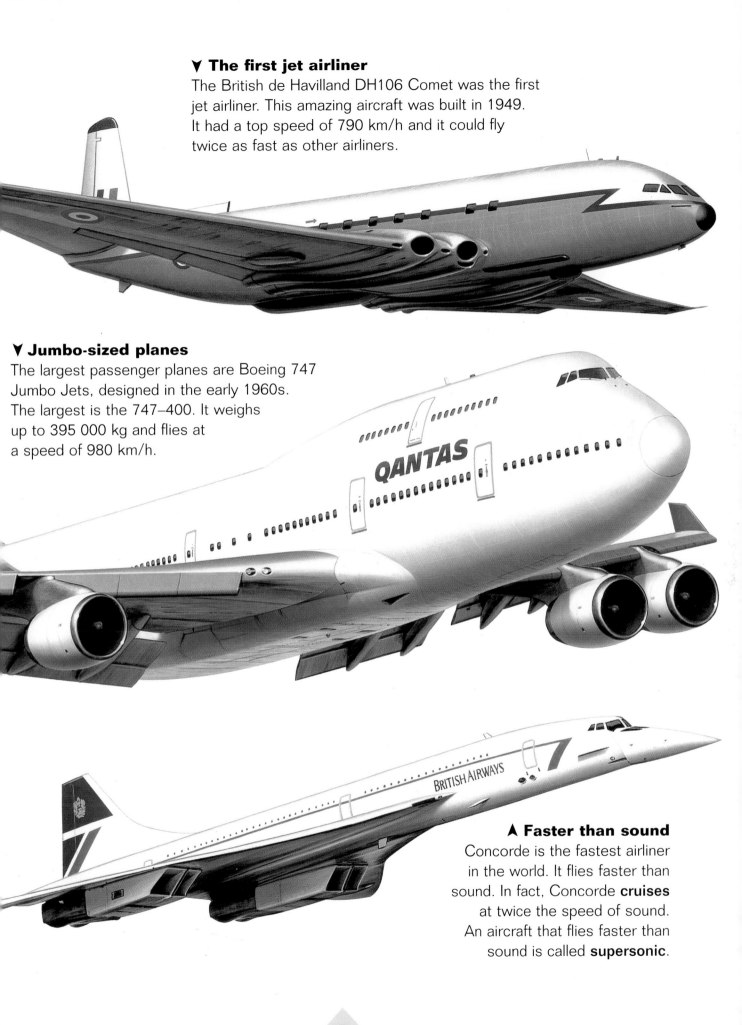

▼ The first jet airliner

The British de Havilland DH106 Comet was the first jet airliner. This amazing aircraft was built in 1949. It had a top speed of 790 km/h and it could fly twice as fast as other airliners.

▼ Jumbo-sized planes

The largest passenger planes are Boeing 747 Jumbo Jets, designed in the early 1960s. The largest is the 747–400. It weighs up to 395 000 kg and flies at a speed of 980 km/h.

QANTAS

BRITISH AIRWAYS

▲ Faster than sound

Concorde is the fastest airliner in the world. It flies faster than sound. In fact, Concorde **cruises** at twice the speed of sound. An aircraft that flies faster than sound is called **supersonic**.

Designing for speed

The shape of an aircraft is a vital part of its design. An aircraft pushes air aside as it flies along. At the same time, air pushes back and slows down the aircraft. This is called air resistance, or **drag**. The faster an aircraft tries to fly, the more air resistance there is. Fast planes are shaped like darts so that they can cut through the air at high speeds. Smoothing out an aircraft's shape so that it slips through the air easily is called streamlining.

Boeing 767
jet airliner

Dash 7
airliner

▼ Folding undercarriage
Most aircraft have a retractable **undercarriage**. After take-off, doors in the **fuselage** and wings open to let the wheels retract, or fold up, inside the plane. Then the doors close and form a smooth streamlined surface.

▲ Swept back for speed
Slow planes like the Dash 7 airliner have wings that stick straight out. Fast jet airliners like the Boeing 767 have wings angled backwards to be more streamlined. The wings of **supersonic** planes like the Dassault Rafale fighter are swept back so far that they form a triangular shape called a **delta wing**.

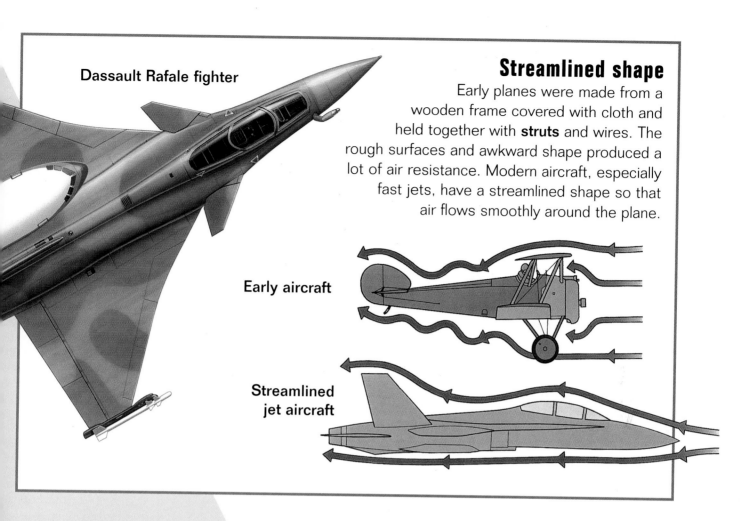

Dassault Rafale fighter

Streamlined shape

Early planes were made from a wooden frame covered with cloth and held together with **struts** and wires. The rough surfaces and awkward shape produced a lot of air resistance. Modern aircraft, especially fast jets, have a streamlined shape so that air flows smoothly around the plane.

Early aircraft

Streamlined jet aircraft

Engine design

A small, light aircraft with a piston engine can fly at a maximum speed of 600 km/h. Heavier and faster planes need a more powerful engine. Airliners and fighters often have jet engines. The fastest jet aircraft fly at 2000–3000 km/h.

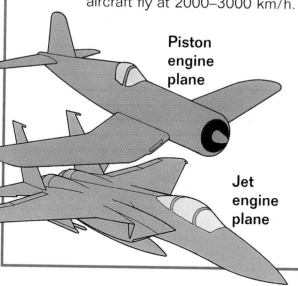

Piston engine plane

Jet engine plane

▲ Increasing the power

Concorde and most fighters use jet engines fitted with **afterburners**. When the pilot turns on the afterburners, fuel is sprayed into the fiery hot gases streaming out of the engine. The fuel burns and produces extra power for take-off or **acceleration**.

On the drawing board

lift

drag

thrust

gravity

An aircraft is a complicated machine. It is built from thousands of parts made from materials such as metal, plastic, glass and rubber. Modern aircraft are designed with the help of computers. This is called computer-aided design. The computer can show a picture of the whole aircraft or any part of it, and turn it around so that the designer can see it from every angle. The BAe Hawk 200 was designed by computer. It is light and extremely fast.

▲ Forces of flight

There are four forces that act on an aircraft when it flies. **Gravity** pulls it down, so wings or spinning rotor blades lift it. Air resistance, or **drag**, slows down the aircraft, so engines produce **thrust** to push it forwards.

BAe Hawk 200

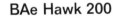

◄ Computer-aided design

Computers speed up the process of designing an aircraft. Designers change and experiment with parts of an aircraft quickly and easily using a computer. The aircraft is changed and improved many times before building work starts.

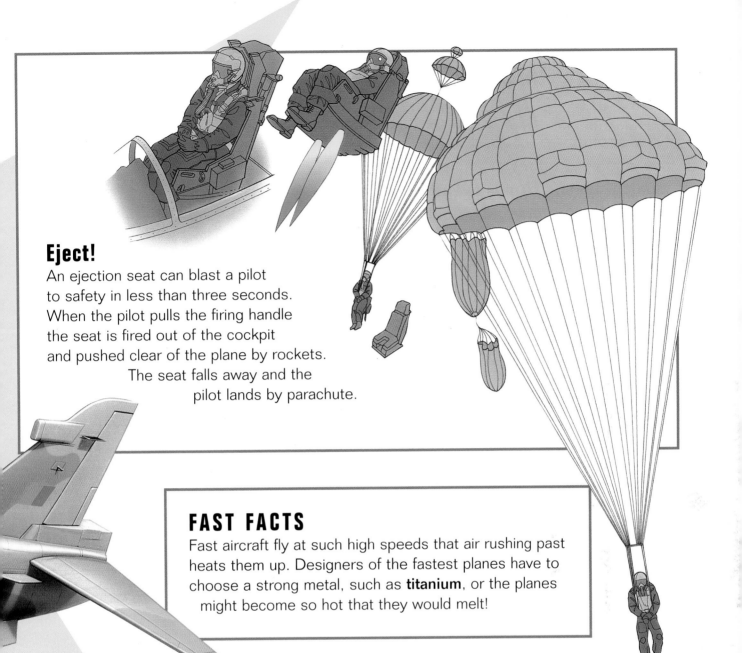

Eject!

An ejection seat can blast a pilot
to safety in less than three seconds.
When the pilot pulls the firing handle
the seat is fired out of the cockpit
and pushed clear of the plane by rockets.
The seat falls away and the
pilot lands by parachute.

FAST FACTS

Fast aircraft fly at such high speeds that air rushing past
heats them up. Designers of the fastest planes have to
choose a strong metal, such as **titanium**, or the planes
might become so hot that they would melt!

On the production line ➤
Computers control the process
of making aircraft parts and
building the finished aircraft.
Many pieces are
welded together,
and computers
make sure that
nothing goes wrong.
It is a quick and
efficient production line.

Will it work?

New aircraft are tested to make sure that they are safe before they are given to air forces or airlines. Testing begins even before the aircraft is built. Computers and models show how each part of the aircraft will work during a flight. When the aircraft is built, test pilots fly it to check that there are no unexpected problems and that it flies exactly as its designers planned.

◄ Computer testing
Computers draw colourful pictures of the new aircraft to show how parts will move in flight. Designers can see which parts have to be strong. This computer image is an engine fan.

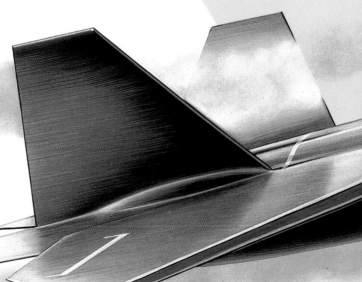

McDonnell Douglas
aircraft testing new engines

◄ Flying test beds
Sometimes a part designed for a new aircraft is tested by building it into another aircraft. An aircraft used in this way is called a flying test bed. It is a good way of testing new engines or trying out a different wing shape.

◀ Early days

In the early days of aircraft, the only way to test a new plane was to fly it. Early planes were slower than most modern cars but they were still very dangerous to fly. The controls were hard to use and the pilot had no protection at all.

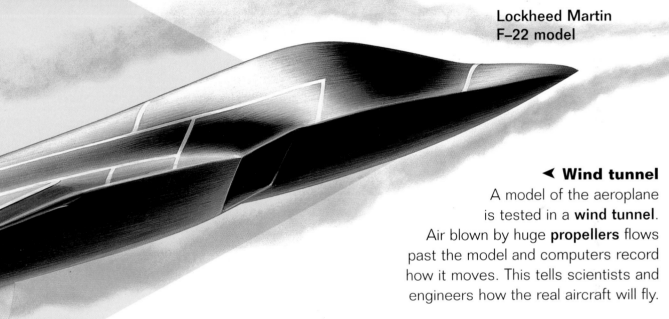

Lockheed Martin F–22 model

◀ Wind tunnel

A model of the aeroplane is tested in a **wind tunnel**. Air blown by huge **propellers** flows past the model and computers record how it moves. This tells scientists and engineers how the real aircraft will fly.

Mach numbers

The speed of fast aircraft is not always measured in kilometres per hour. The **speed of sound** is called Mach 1. The fastest planes can fly at more than Mach 3, three times the speed of sound. The Mach speed system was named after Ernst Mach (1838-1916), a scientist who studied how air flows around objects moving at high speeds.

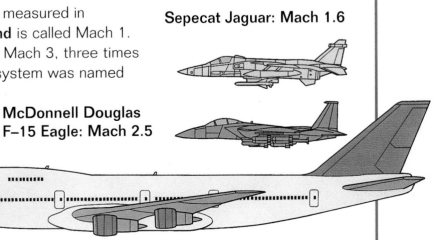

Sepecat Jaguar: Mach 1.6

McDonnell Douglas F–15 Eagle: Mach 2.5

Boeing 747: Mach 0.9

Engine power

Fast aircraft need powerful engines to propel them through the air. Concorde and a few of the fastest fighters are powered by a jet engine called a turbojet. Most airliners and fighters are powered by a jet engine called a turbofan. All jet engines work in the same way. Air is sucked inside and heated by burning fuel. The heat makes the air expand so that it rushes out of the engine as a jet of hot gas.

Panavia Tornado

Rocket-powered fighter ➤
The Messerschmitt Me163 Komet was the first rocket-powered fighter. In 1941 it broke the world air speed record when it flew at 1004 km/h. Komets were dangerous planes to fly because they had a nasty habit of exploding on landing!

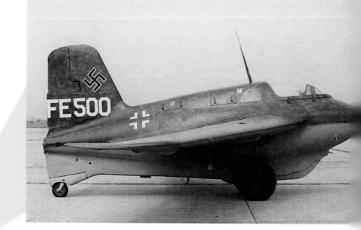

▲ Flying to the limit

The X–15 was a US rocket plane that flew to the limits of the Earth's **atmosphere** many times in the 1960s. Its rocket engine boosted it to speeds of more than 7000 km/h. The design of the X–15 was used to help build the US **space shuttle**.

Burning fuel ➤
Fuel inside an engine can only burn when **oxygen** is added. Jet engines suck in oxygen from the air, but in space there is no air to use. This means that rockets have to carry their own oxygen supply.

Rocket flies upwards

fuel

oxygen

hot gases out

How jet engines work

➤ Turbojet

A turbojet sucks in air and compresses, or squeezes, it. Burning fuel produces hot gases. The gases flow through the **turbine** and make it spin.

air in

fuel in

hot gases out

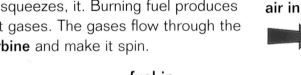

air in

fuel in

hot gases out

turbine

◄ Turbofan

A turbofan works like a turbojet, except that some of the air sucked in by a large fan at the front flows around the outside of the engine.

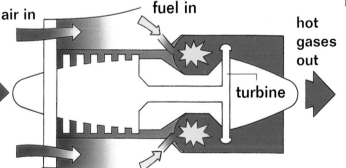

turbine

➤ Ramjet

The simplest jet engine is the ramjet. It has no moving parts. The speed of the aircraft 'rams' air into the engine.

air in

fuel in

hot gases out

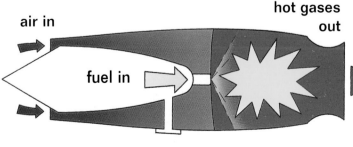

Supersonic flight

Aircraft that can fly faster than the **speed of sound** have a streamlined shape to help them fly at high speed. The wings are thin with sharp edges and swept back so much that they sometimes join the tail to form a **delta wing**. The body of the aircraft is slim, its engines are narrow and its nose ends in a sharp point. The aircraft speeds through the air without wasting fuel and engine power in overcoming air resistance.

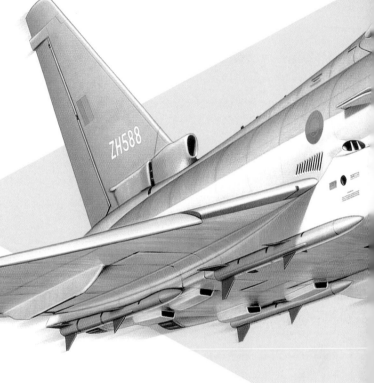

Eurofighter EFA 2000

What is a sonic boom?

When an aircraft flies faster than sound, air in front of it does not move aside fast enough. It piles up in front of the plane and forms a shock wave which is like the wave of water that builds up in front of a ship. The shock wave spreads out like ripples of water. When it reaches the ground it makes a loud booming noise. This is called a sonic boom. You can hear it as the aircraft passes over your head.

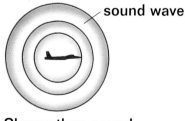

sound wave

Slower than sound

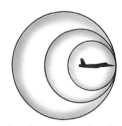

At the speed of sound

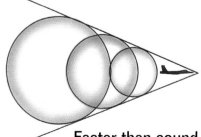

Faster than sound

◄ A supersonic first

The first plane to fly faster than sound was the American Bell X–1. On 14 October 1947 the bullet-shaped orange plane was dropped from a B–29 bomber. The X–1's pilot, Charles Yeager, fired its rocket engine and reached a speed of Mach 1.07. Yeager had become the first supersonic pilot.

FAST FACTS

Concorde flies from London Heathrow airport to New York's J F Kennedy airport in under three-and-a-half hours. To do this it changes **time zones**, which means that passengers arrive in New York more than an hour earlier than they left London.

▼ Supersonic engines

Jet engines cannot work with air flowing through at supersonic speeds. Concorde has a special **channel** leading to the engine to slow down the air. Computer-controlled **ramps** move up and down to slow the speed of air from Mach 2 to only Mach 0.5.

▲ A drooping nose

Concorde's streamlined nose, or 'snoot', is the best shape for flying faster than sound, but it means that the pilot does not have a good view downwards. As Concorde comes in to land, the nose tips down, or droops, so that the pilot can see the runway.

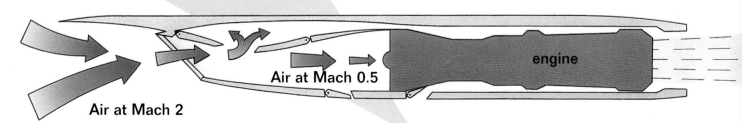

Air at Mach 0.5

engine

Air at Mach 2

Fast and furious

Fighter planes are the fastest aircraft. Their job is to catch and attack enemy aircraft, so they must be quick and well-armed. They have to be able to turn, climb or dive at high speeds. The McDonnell Douglas F–15 Eagle is one of the world's top fighters. This amazing plane climbs at up to 250 metres per second to a height of more than 18 000 metres. It flies at 2655 km/h, armed with a gun and up to eight **missiles**.

▲ Putting on weight
A fully armed fighter is much heavier than an unarmed plane so it cannot fly at full speed. The missiles and **pylons** are all streamlined to cut down air resistance.

Swing-wing fighters
Straight wings are best for take-off and landing, but swept back wings are better for high-speed flight. Swing-wing fighters have wings that swivel out for take-off and landing, then swivel backwards to form a **delta wing** for **supersonic** flight.

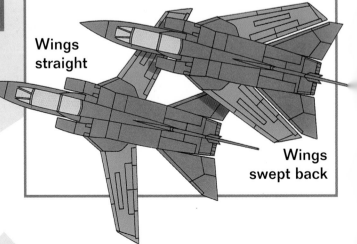

Wings
straight

Wings
swept back

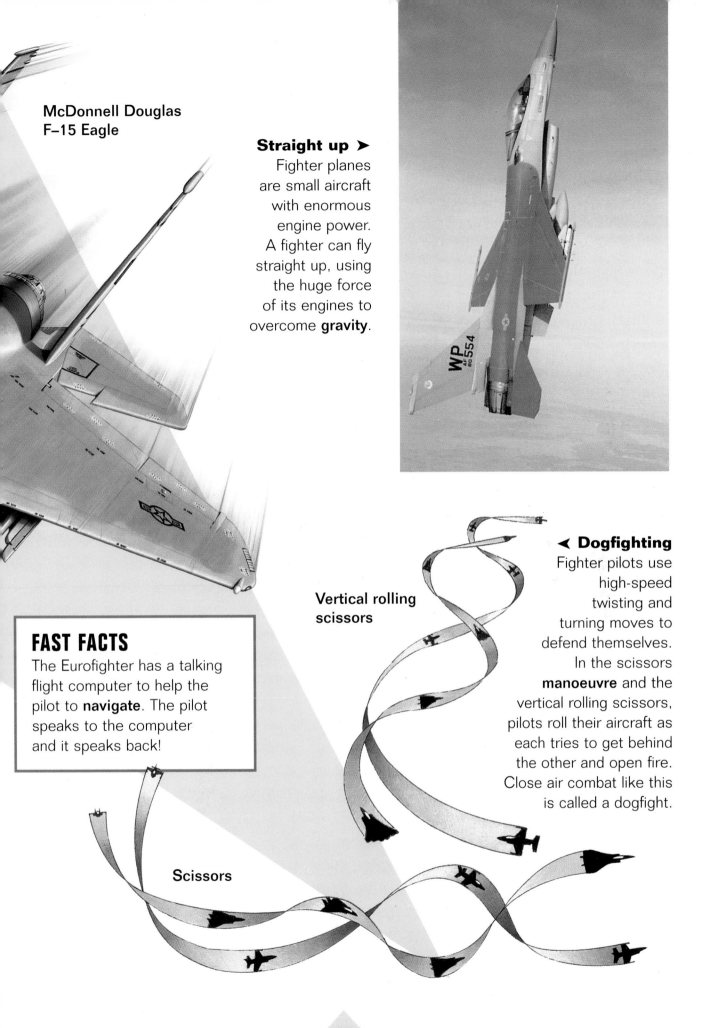

**McDonnell Douglas
F–15 Eagle**

Straight up ➤
Fighter planes
are small aircraft
with enormous
engine power.
A fighter can fly
straight up, using
the huge force
of its engines to
overcome **gravity**.

◄ Dogfighting
Fighter pilots use
high-speed
twisting and
turning moves to
defend themselves.
In the scissors
manoeuvre and the
vertical rolling scissors,
pilots roll their aircraft as
each tries to get behind
the other and open fire.
Close air combat like this
is called a dogfight.

**Vertical rolling
scissors**

FAST FACTS
The Eurofighter has a talking
flight computer to help the
pilot to **navigate**. The pilot
speaks to the computer
and it speaks back!

Scissors

Flying to win

The first air races were organized in the early days of flying to help to develop faster aircraft. Air races are still held today for fun. Many racing planes are Second World War fighters that have been rebuilt. A good racing plane is small and light, with a very powerful engine. Planes race against each other in fast and exciting contests.

P–38 Lightning

▲ First to Australia
In 1934 the first ever air race from England to Australia took place. Three de Havilland DH88 Comets were specially designed and built to take part. One of the Comets, called Gloucester House, won the race. It covered 18 240 kilometres in 70 hours 54 minutes at an average speed of 256 km/h.

▲ The Reno Air Races
Some of the best racing planes can be seen at America's famous Reno Air Races. Many different kinds of aircraft take part, but the most exciting and popular events are the races for Second World War planes. Every year these old warplanes are improved so that they fly even faster.

Racing over water

One of the most famous aircraft races was the Schneider Trophy seaplane race. Planes flew seven times round the 48 km route over the sea. The crowd had a good view from the nearby beach. The race route was marked out by poles called pylons. The planes flew round each pylon.

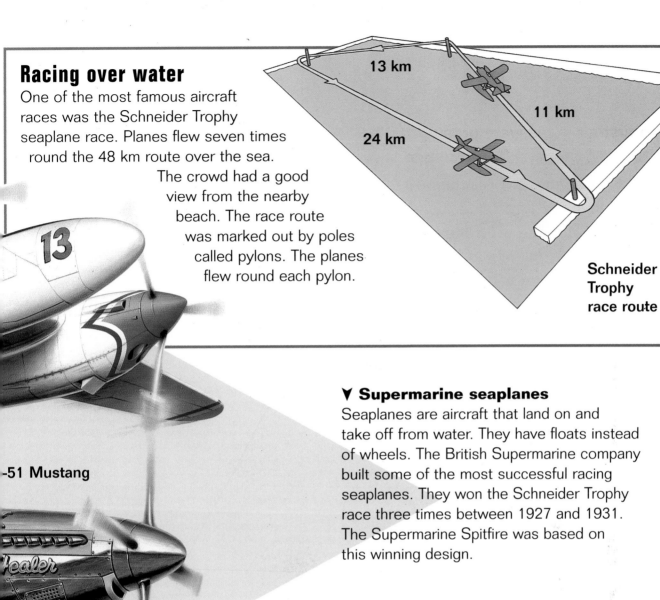

13 km

11 km

24 km

Schneider Trophy race route

-51 Mustang

▼ Supermarine seaplanes

Seaplanes are aircraft that land on and take off from water. They have floats instead of wheels. The British Supermarine company built some of the most successful racing seaplanes. They won the Schneider Trophy race three times between 1927 and 1931. The Supermarine Spitfire was based on this winning design.

FAST FACTS

Just before a race, some planes are polished with an electric polisher. This reduces **drag** so that they can fly as fast as possible. It just might make the difference between winning and losing a race.

Blasting into space

When a spacecraft is launched, it must reach a speed of at least 28 000 km/h to stay in space. If it reaches 40 000 km/h it can leave the Earth and travel towards other planets. The only engine that has enough power for this is the rocket. A **space shuttle** has three rocket engines in its tail. They are supplied with fuel from a large red tank attached to the shuttle. There are also two **booster rockets** to give extra power needed for take-off.

▲ Boosting the shuttle

At take-off, booster rockets burn like huge fireworks. When the space shuttle reaches a height of 50 km, the booster rockets fall into the Atlantic Ocean. They are collected by ships and refuelled to launch another space shuttle.

Fuel tank falls away

Boosters fall away

Shuttle in space

Shuttle re-enters atmosphere

▶ Return to Earth

When a space shuttle re-enters the **atmosphere** it has to slow down from more than 20 times the **speed of sound** to 350 km/h before it lands. It does this by flying along a zig zag path, slowing down all the time. It lands on a runway like an airliner.

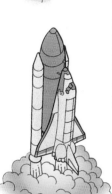

Take-off

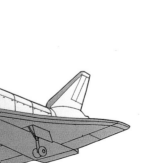

Shuttle lands

FAST FACTS

The space shuttle is covered with 27 000 glassy tiles. They are specially designed to protect the shuttle and the crew inside from the incredible heat of re-entry.

► Launching a rocket

Satellites are usually launched into space by rockets. A rocket is tall and slim with a bullet-shaped nose. It is powered through the atmosphere by motors in its tail. The rocket is controlled by computers, which make sure it stays on course.

Changing direction in space

A space shuttle has more than 40 tiny rocket **thrusters** in its nose and tail. They point in all directions and are fired to change the direction of the spacecraft. Two extra **manoeuvring** engines in the tail are used to make bigger changes in speed and height.

Tail thrusters

Nose thrusters

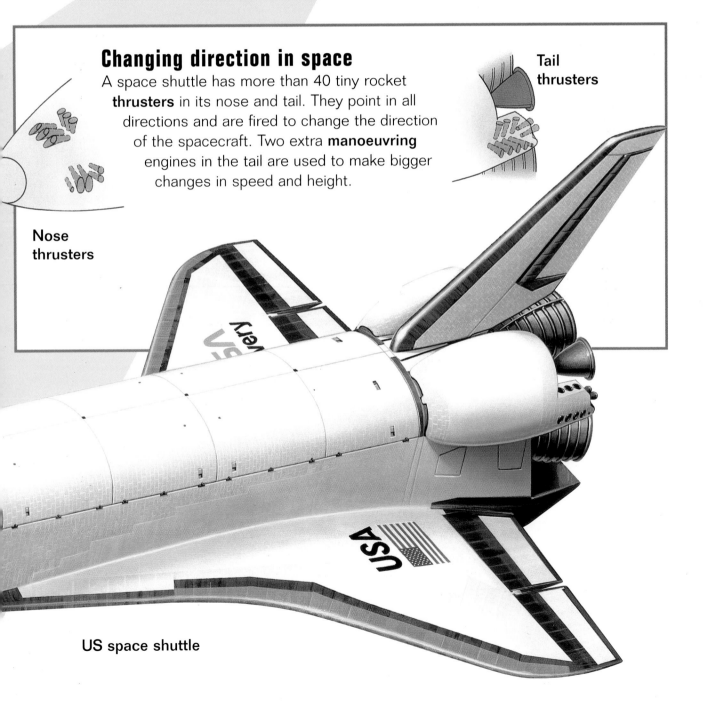

US space shuttle

Spinning wings

Helicopters are propelled through the air in a different way from aircraft with wings. Long thin rotor blades spin above a helicopter and push air downwards. This means that the helicopter takes off and lands vertically. The world speed helicopter record was set in 1986 when a British Westland Lynx reached 400 km/h. Even the fastest helicopters are slower than aircraft with wings, but new designs like the Tiltrotor may change this.

▲ Super strength
The Sikorsky S–80 Super Stallion is one of the world's fastest and strongest helicopters. It has three powerful jet engines called **turboshafts** and a seven-bladed main rotor. It flies at a speed of 315 km/h.

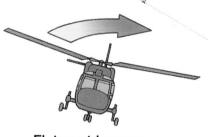

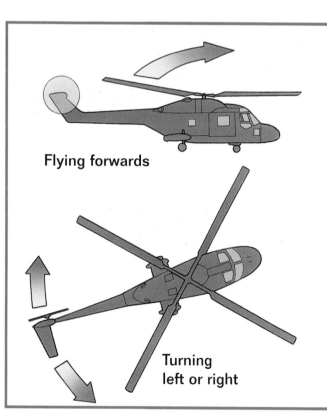

Flying forwards

Flying sideways

Turning left or right

Steering and turning

To turn a helicopter from side to side the pilot uses a control stick to lift the rotor blades on one side and lower them on the other. The blades can also be tilted down at the front and up at the back to move the helicopter forwards. The small tail rotor helps the helicopter to turn to the left or the right.

▼ Glass blades

Many modern helicopters have very strong rotor blades made from materials like **carbon** and glass. The materials are mixed to strengthen each other. This mixture is called a **composite**.

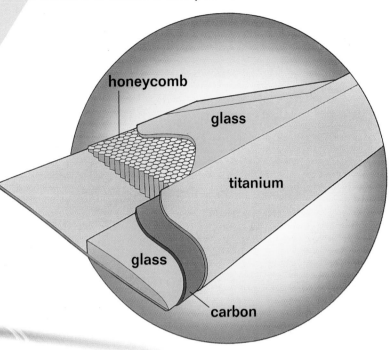

honeycomb

glass

titanium

glass

carbon

Westland Lynx

Tilting rotors ➤

The new Tiltrotor aircraft takes off vertically like a helicopter and then flies like an aeroplane. Long **propellers** lift it off the ground. Then the huge engines tilt forwards and wings lift the aircraft. The Tiltrotor flies at twice the speed of an ordinary helicopter.

Staying in control

A pilot steers an aircraft using controls in the cockpit. These are linked to parts of the wings and tail called control surfaces. When the control surfaces move, the air flowing round the plane presses against them. This makes the aircraft change direction. The fastest aircraft have computerized controls in the wings and tail because the force of air pressing against the surfaces is too strong for the pilot to move the controls by hand.

▲ Computers in the cockpit
Modern aircraft are fitted with computers that **monitor** the plane's speed, engines and the sky around. The computers are linked to screens in the cockpit.

▼ Control surfaces
There are three types of control surfaces. **Elevators** in the tail make the plane climb or dive. **Ailerons** in the wings make it roll. A **rudder** in the tail makes it turn left or right. Aircraft with a **delta wing** have panels in the wing called **elevons** that do the job of both elevators and ailerons.

McDonnell Douglas
F/A–18 Hornets

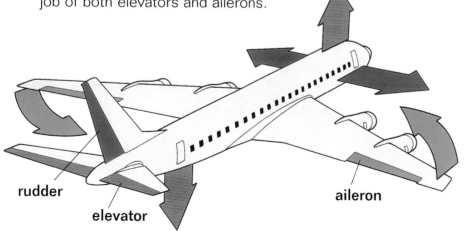

rudder

elevator

aileron

▲ Tumbling fighters
Some fighters are made unsteady so that they can turn, dive and climb quickly. Computers make changes to the control surfaces many times every second to keep the plane flying smoothly. Many computerized fighters are used in exciting air displays.

Head-up displays

Helmet-mounted display

▲ Making flying easier

A head-up display projects flight information on to a glass plate in front of the pilot, so that he or she doesn't have to look down at computer screens. Helmet-mounted displays are now being developed. These show information on the pilot's **visor** to make it even easier to see.

▲ Formation flying

A fighter pilot must be able to **navigate** well to stay in control. Military aircraft fly in tight **formations** to protect each other. The clear **canopy** of this Tornado GR1A gives the pilot a good view of the other planes.

Record breakers

Some types of aircraft can reach amazing speeds. In 1967 the X–15 rocket plane flew at 7274 km/h when it was launched by being dropped from a B–52 bomber. When the US **space shuttle** re-enters the Earth's **atmosphere** it travels at more than 25 000 km/h. The fastest aircraft to take off and land under its own power is the Lockheed SR–71 Blackbird. In 1976 it flew at 3529 km/h and set a new world air speed record.

The fastest airliner ➤
Concorde is still the world's fastest airliner. Only 20 were built and 12 are in regular service. They fly up to 100 passengers across the Atlantic Ocean at twice the **speed of sound**. This takes less than four hours.

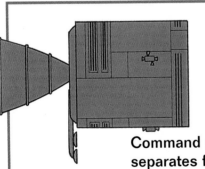
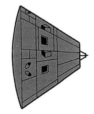

Command module separates from spacecraft

Module re-enters atmosphere

The fastest humans
The fastest that people have ever travelled is 39 897 km/h. The **command module** of the Apollo 10 spacecraft reached this speed as it returned to Earth on 26 May 1969. It covered 11 km every second and became very hot. The blunt end of the tiny cone-shaped craft was covered with a **heat shield** to protect it.

Module lands

**Lockheed
SR–71 Blackbird**

▲ Fastest in combat

The fastest combat aircraft is the Russian MiG–25. It flies at 3300 km/h, faster than Mach 3. Most of the MiG–25 is made of steel. The nose and front edges of the wings are made of **titanium** because they heat up so much in flight.

Above
1370°C

Below
315°C

◄ Top secret!

Lockheed SR–71 Blackbirds were once the USA's most successful spy planes. They carried out many top secret missions without ever being **intercepted**. Two are still used by the US space agency **NASA** for high-speed, high-**altitude** research. They fly so fast that the front edges of the wings heat up to 430°C.

◄ Super transport

When the space shuttle re-enters the Earth's atmosphere it is travelling more than ten times faster than Concorde. This diagram shows how hot the shuttle is at this speed. The lightest areas are the hottest.

FAST FACTS

Charles Yeager managed to become the world's first **supersonic** pilot in October 1947 even though he had two broken ribs from a riding accident!

Shaping the future

Designers are always working on faster aircraft for the future. Research centres and aircraft manufacturers around the world are developing aircraft that will replace Concorde. Scientists and engineers study ways of increasing engine power and speed, making better materials and cutting down on air pollution. As they find answers to these problems, amazing aircraft take shape on their computer screens.

➤ Back to front wings
One of the oddest looking ideas for future fighters is to give them forward swept wings. The wings are made from strong **composite** materials so that they do not break off during flight. The Grumman X–29 was built to try out this idea.

◄ Faster than ever

Some designers are planning to build planes that can fly at speeds of more than Mach 5. These are called **hypersonic** aircraft. The body of the aircraft is shaped like one big wing, which makes it look very strange.

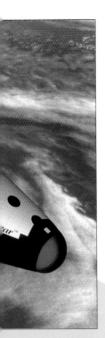

◄ A new Concorde

European aircraft manufacturers are working on a new **supersonic** aircraft that will be twice as fast as Concorde. It does not need a 'droop snoot' to help the pilot see the ground below. Instead, the pilot has a television screen in the cockpit that shows a clear view of the sky around.

▲ Invisible aircraft

Some military aircraft are designed so that they do not show up on enemy radar screens. They are called stealth aircraft. The newest stealth fighter in the US Air Force is the Lockheed Martin F–22. It zooms in on enemy planes without being seen.

► Future fighter

A new fighter aircraft for the 21st century is being developed in the USA. It is called the Joint Strike Fighter and it will be faster and more difficult to spot on enemy **radar screens** than any other fighter. So far it only exists as a computer-generated picture.

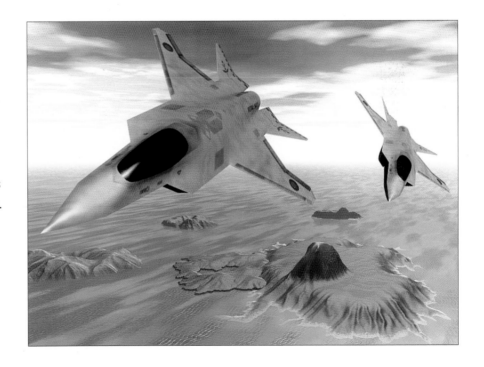

Glossary

acceleration
Going faster and faster.

afterburner
A part of a jet engine that sprays fuel into the hot gases coming out of the engine. This produces extra power.

ailerons
Movable panels in an aircraft wing. When one aileron lifts up, the aileron in the opposite wing moves down and the plane rolls over to one side.

altitude
The height of an aircraft above the ground.

atmosphere
The gases that are all around the Earth or any other planet. We need these gases to live and breathe.

booster rocket
An extra rocket used to help launch a spacecraft. The space shuttle uses two booster rockets that fall away when their fuel runs out.

canopy
The see-through cover of an aircraft cockpit.

carbon
A black substance. Diamond, charcoal and pencil leads are made of carbon. Carbon is used in aircraft building because it can be very strong and it does not melt at high temperatures.

cargo
Goods carried by a vehicle.

channel
A tube that gas or liquid flows through. A channel in Concorde's jet engine is shaped to slow down the air passing through it.

command module
The small cone-shaped end of the Apollo spacecraft where the crew sits. When the astronauts return to Earth, the command module separates from the rest of the spacecraft and parachutes into the ocean.

composite
A material made from two or more different materials. A composite is very strong.

cruise
To fly at a steady speed. An aircraft's cruising speed is lower than its top speed.

delta wing
An aircraft wing swept back so far that it joins the body to make a triangular shape.

drag
Drag, or air resistance, is the force that slows an aircraft down.

elevators
Movable panels in an aircraft tail. When the elevators lift up, the tail drops, the nose rises and the plane climbs. When the elevators move down, the nose drops and the plane dives.

elevons
Movable panels in the delta wing of a supersonic aircraft. They do the same job as elevators and ailerons on an ordinary aircraft.

formation
A group of aircraft flying together. Military planes fly in formation to protect each other.

fuselage
The main body of an aircraft.

gravity
A force that holds everything down on the ground. The heavier something is, the stronger its pull of gravity is.

heat shield
The covering on a spacecraft that protects it from high temperatures.

hypersonic
Speeds of more than five times the speed of sound.

intercept
To stop enemy aircraft from reaching their target by sending fighters to catch them. These fighters are called interceptors.

manoeuvre
A controlled movement of an aircraft. A pilot has to be very skilful to carry out difficult manoeuvres.

missile
A rocket-powered weapon that flies towards a target and explodes.

monitor
To check for problems or danger. Aircraft have computers to monitor the plane and the sky around.

NASA
National Aeronautics and Space Administration. This is the organization that runs space projects in the United States.

navigate
To give directions for a plane. The member of the crew who does this is called the navigator. Modern aircraft use computers to navigate.

oxygen
A gas in the air around us. We need oxygen to breathe and engines need oxygen to burn fuel.

propeller
Long blades that spin to push, or propel, an aircraft through the air.

pylon
The part of an aircraft that holds an engine or weapon in place underneath the plane.

radar screen
A screen that looks like a television screen or computer screen. It shows the positions of aircraft that are flying too far away for the pilot to see.

ramp
A sloping surface. Ramps in Concorde's engines move up and down to slow down air as it flows into the engine.

rudder
The part of an aircraft's tail that moves to the left or right to turn the aircraft from side to side.

satellite
An object that travels round and round a planet. The Earth's moon and moons that circle other planets are satellites. A spacecraft that travels round and round a planet is also called a satellite.

space shuttle
A spacecraft designed to be used again and again. It carries astronauts into space and back to Earth.

speed of sound
Sound travels through the air at about 1225 km/h near the ground. In colder air high above the ground, the speed of sound falls to about 1062 km/h. The speed of sound is also called Mach 1.

strut
A stiff rod that holds aircraft parts in place.

supersonic
Faster than the speed of sound.

thrust
The force created by a propeller or an engine that pushes an aircraft forwards.

thruster
A small rocket engine. It is used to make tiny changes to a spacecraft's position.

time zone
An area of the world that has a certain time. There are 24 time zones in the world. If you travel from one time zone to another, you have to change your watch because the time changes.

titanium
A strong, light metal. It is used to make fast aircraft.

turbine
Part of a jet engine. A turbine is a disc with blades fixed around the edge. As hot gases rush through a jet engine, they hit the blades and make the turbine spin.

turboshaft
A helicopter engine. It is connected to a shaft, or rod, that turns the rotor blades.

undercarriage
An aircraft's wheels.

visor
The see-through part of a helmet that covers the pilot's face.

weld
To join two pieces of metal or plastic by melting them together.

wind tunnel
A tunnel with a strong wind flowing through it. A model of a new aircraft is placed inside the wind tunnel. Designers watch how the model moves in the wind to find out how the real aircraft will fly.

Index